DEATHDOUBLEDACTYL

WINNER OF THE TRANSCONTINENTAL POETRY AWARD

DEATHDOUBLEDACTYL

SHANNON HAMANN

PAVEMENT SAW PRESS
OHIO

Editor & Interior layout: David Baratier
Duck Logo: Joe Napora
Cover Art: Attila Richard Lukacs *Painting of Shannon*
Cover Design: Jared Bangert

We would like to thank the editors of the following journals in which some of these poems first appeared, sometimes in earlier versions: *The Atlanta Review, The Bluffs Reader, Borderlands: Texas Poetry Review, The Colorado Review, Cover Magazine, Free Lunch, The Georgia State University Review, The Gettysburg Review, The Harbinger, The Hawaii Review, International Poetry Review, The Madison Review, Tribes, Many Mountains Moving, Maryland Poetry Review, The Massachusetts Review, Mockingbird, Mudfish, The New York Quarterly, Nimrod, Pavement, Slingshot, Visions International,* and *Zyzzyva.* "Redemption" appeared in the anthology *The Best of Writers at Work.* Some of these poems also appeared in the limited edition collection *L'immaginazione violenta* by Italian publisher Edizioni Cadmo.

Pavement Saw Press
321 Empire Street
Montpelier OH 43543
http://pavementsaw.org

Full length books are available through the publisher or through:
SPD / 1341 Seventh St / Berkeley, CA 94710 / 800.869.7553
Literary journals and chapbooks are only available through the publisher

Winner of the Transcontinental Poetry Award
for an outstanding first-book collection of poetry or prose. We read yearly from June 1st until August 15th. Send SASE for more information.

Pavement Saw Press is a not for profit organization, any donations are greatly appreciated and are considerered as charitable tax donations under section 501 (c) (3) of the federal tax code.

CONTENTS

Art is individualism, and individualism is a disturbing and disintegrating force.

There lies its immense value. For what it seeks is to disturb monotony of type, slavery of custom, tyranny of habit, and the reduction of man to the level of a machine.

—Oscar Wilde

EASTER

Death is stubborn this year,
and by now has shed all its christmassy vanity.
The sky is painted a plain Jane shade of heather and the mercury is shy—
Spring has come only to the calendar,
but this is rebirth North Dakota-style:
The newborn is born ugly, shivering or born dead
or not born at all—
                    all just to illustrate the ignorance of certainty?

An iced-over stew of last year's leaves lines the gutters.
Last summer's wishes for temperature plunges come true.
It is colder for expecting warmth.
Buds don't bud.
Daffodils don't daff.
Heather doesn't doesn't. Tomato
plants panic and die and shrivel and rot and go away.

It is the time one finds a spot of blood on an egg
and one is tired of seeing one's breath.
My sister writes she's been crying a lot lately.
Trees don't fatten.
Birch bark flakes and birds huddle and cry.
The cat doesn't shed—he knows.
The water in the glass an elderly neighbor leaves her teeth in
has cooled cooler still overnight and the set of teeth
shocks her gums in the morning and sends a chill through her body.
She dies.
            Nothing blooms.

                            Not nothing, but less yet—
            there, in the shame-filled room,
            spilled children, there, at the writing table
            the muse implodes—

It is the time when a young man's fancy turns to thoughts that would
make a whore puke.

9

On Easter, my own grandmother dies.
I cook a plum jam-glazed and unlucky turkey
(who does not see from the standpoint of Christian Orthodoxy)
which friends do not make it over to eat. This is snow country.
I write my sister to tell her that I've been crying a lot lately.

God is crucified, dead, and buried.
The ground is frozen but He needs no gravedigger.
God is cruel. He prefers to sleep.
God is a coward. He prefers to sleep.
For His is the kingdom of indifference,
And ours is frustration,
                                despair,
                                        and enclosure
                                                forever.
On Easter,
The ground is a gizzard gravy gray-brown .
The only green grass is Easter Grass
from Eggsville, USA (discounted at Reliable Drug).
Buds don't bud.
Cocoons don't open.
It is the time when everything is restless.
It is the time when we hear the wind wander under the window,
and we whisper back, "Defrost, defrost. Awaken,"
and we hear in our minds
the tiptoe step between self-sabotage and self-murder,
and we hear the choice echo, "which one? Which one?"
It is the time when you realize, my God,
death is the meat and potatoes; life is gravy.
A squirrel throws itself against the back porch screen door
and you realize
It is time to take everything you ever thought and stop thinking it.
A deer starves
And we hear the mind.

TRANSUBSTANTIATION

A friend of a friend of a friend lived so near a bakery
she could not make unleavened bread:
the yeast infiltrated every inch of air
                                    like the Holy Spirit.
In each breath you take there is likely to be

a molecule from Christ's last breath. Last breaths
disperse and disperse:
even on the freshest spring morning
the first whispers of the Final Solution
fill your lungs. And particles
from the curses of the tortured
and the torturers fill a clown's balloon.
The breath from a sibilant from a word in one of
der Führer's speeches nestles in a bubble in a Communion wafer
or a champagne bubble(*Happy New Year!*).
Twelve million last breaths fuel the winds across Europe.
The dead are alive
in breezes and pear trees.
History surrounds us like laughter.
This is transubstantiation, and it is utterly real.
Pieces of Christ are in your cocaine,
        your bath water, your birthday cake, your dime novel, the ink of
your lottery ticket,
        your virus, the tapes that keep your spit curls in place, and you—
They cover you primordially like a variety of ivy
like Munch's red vine.
Wine becomes blood.
Ideas become ink.
This is not fancy—it's science.

As a child, there was one thought that would stop me cold:
Why isn't there nothing at all?
                            Not just

no people or no world,
but no sun, no universe, no single atom, zero.

And still more chilling is the thought that someday this question will be
what people think moot means because
our Waterloo will find us —
                              Chatterton's arsenic, Foucault's AIDS,
Plath's oven,
Your Calvary will knock —
                              Flannery O'Connor's lupus, the liver cancer
of Hans Christian Andersen, Dickens's stroke
                    (*Knock knock*)
I'm so afraid.
              (Who's there?)
Even Lazarus died for good.

When I am only bones or less
who will eat me as the scale of an anchovy
in a salad?
What I'm really asking is,
may I please have some more?

Recently in Los Angeles a man drove himself to the emergency
room with an axe in his cranium,
walked up to the counter,
and dropped dead.
It's true what they say about truth.
It took fourteen tries to decapitate Mary
Stuart. After a whack that only exposed her brain
like a pod dehiscing, she cried out, "Sweet Jesus!"

Did Christ on the cross cry out for Mary?

Did He cry out for His grandma,
                            "Anne! *Anne!*"
                                          ?

or mutter the names of His brothers...*Jimmy...Simon*.?

No: His speech was unpeopled. He said (according to the gospel of John)
simply, "It is done."

But in the gospel of Matthew He beseeches, "My God,
My God, why hast Thou forsaken Me?"

But in the gospel of Mark

as He bleeds from His brown tiara on His bleached rack,

absolutely nothing

comes out His piehole.

The Kite

A boy on a hill flew a kite his father had given him.
What a beautiful Sunday. The grass had returned
And was thicker and greener. Rabbits wandered
Fearlessly about. Fields were fields again
On the French countryside. Mother's hair had grown back.
It wasn't Spring but a spring of sorts.
Death had fled, sated. Trees shook away sleep.
The odd stares were less odd. The baker
Said to Mother, "What's past is past." And the butcher
Included a little extra fat for the boy.
Soap was allowed in the house again,
And the dogs were no longer given coffee
On the new moon. There was money too—not much
But some—and Mother spoke now and then finally
But never of Papa. Parcels came from relatives
Who from that distance said they understood.

The kite had come one day. Papa had wanted
Him to have it, the relative wrote.
It was a fine kite—not made from paper or fabric
But a light, soft leather.
And as soon as the day was suitable and work was done,
The boy freed the heirloom from its box and let the sky
Pull it away until barely a meter of slack remained.
The dora[1] –kite pitched and turned so high above the hill
It had a good start on Paradise.
                          To look down from
That point would reveal a magnificent spread—
The village and far beyond. The church to the west
Was set against a field of tombs, and those
Who still believed filed out.
                          In the east,
Past Blood Creek, beyond two abandoned cottages,

---

[1] Greek prefix meaning hide

Beyond the acreage owned by the bloodless Schmidts,
A family of ghosts had returned to their home:
The mother ran her hands
Along the smooth, cold
Walls of the corridor
                    (Because when you're a ghost
                    You feel feverish).
Outside the father pried
Turtles from their shells
                              (For soup they cannot eat).
Dogs chase the ugly child
Into the mint patch—
                    The beautiful child is watching.

Walking up the hill itself was a solemn, solitary
Figure dressed in uniform.
                         It moved with a quick gait
As it approached the boy. The head was carried tucked
Under one arm so that when the boy turned to face the
Figure and then turned his head away and then turned it
Back again and uttered, "Papa," he was for the first time
Eye to eye with his father.
                         "Is it true?" the boy asked.
"They say you were not a conventional soldier."
The kite careened and the cord ripped at his fleshy palms.
Papa said, "They persecute you because I am German."
"And Mother, they called her 'un collabo'," said the boy.
"All women are collaborators," Papa said. "Your mother
Did nothing." The kite rattled and swooped and knifed
At the blue. "Then it's true," said the boy.
His hand bled.
                    "Ah, Dora[2] " Papa said fondly. The kite

---

[2] A concentration camp in southwestern Germany

Swerved and somersaulted. The cord cut deeper.
"What we did there, while reprehensible,
Was not uninteresting.
                After all, beauty is all we have."
"Beauty!" scoffed the boy. "There is no beauty
In human suffering."

            Papa said, "There is only beauty
In human suffering.
           It was sublime, a heaven on earth
To which the heaven where I now reside cannot compare.
If all of human history were a single week, this was
Our Saturday night out.
              Think of the shiver you felt
When you tore into your first blood orange that Christmas
Or the bliss when skinning rabbits—
              The hankering
To relive that shiver again and again, to multiply it,
To see, to touch that which the flesh conceals, to hear
The hollers no opera can duplicate, to bathe in the blood
Of virgins, to participate in what will henceforward be
Seen as an occasion for poetry...it
             It overwhelms!
It comes slowly, it comes like sleep, but it [nonsense words]."
The kite trembled and made eights. The boy winced
And said, "You are decadent.
           You've lost."
"No," Papa said, "we've won. You'll see—
From now on the world will be a world of images."

Papa turned and walked away, and the cruciform frame
Of the kite snapped, and the legacy flapped and fell
And rose, and the tattooed kite
Bows from its thank you thank you heights

God says, "I enjoy flying
in the face of fairness."

Even the poorest neighborhood looks like a jewel from an airplane at
night.

American Airlines flight 191, Chicago to Los Angeles,
a gift from Mr. Schade to his beautiful wife
and two little girls.

How aliens must see us:

>   The earthlings go into a building and get dirty pieces of paper. These
buildings, there's one on top of another. They've had to build piggy-back because
their planet is so small, and they're so slow. They go into another building. Big
square holes in all these buildings. Here they put hot stuff into an orifice. Cold
liquids too. Same orifice. Once more those dirty pieces of paper. They give them
to the bringer of hot stuff and cold liquids. What does it all mean?

This is how I see poetry.

I imagine flight 191
from which a tiny car is a zipper
zipping together two patchwork quilts—
a boring magazine, hunger,
one of the engines falls off.
Passengers grab each other, scream,
a woman in row seven says, "I love you"
to her husband who responds,
"I've never loved you…"
"…so much" is lost in the explosion
which incinerates 200 passengers,
200 and change, Chicagoan upon Chicagoan.
Aground, a skeleton hand clutches a former cocktail.
A complimentary peppermint melts in a burning mouth.

Hiroshima Diary

Even here in my neighborhood of concrete
above rice paddies, east and west
greet each other
casually. Mozart spills from
some badly-tuned piano
while ancient women
bent at the waist like sevens
(already leaning into the grave)
gaze up at me (six feet and blond)
as if I were a demon.
Children chirp hello, "Herro!"
They think I am from television, a hero
                              except on August 6
in Hiroshima (I am kicked by a crone in kimono).

This is the way things are:
Love and hate swirled into a taffy. For

example, at the place I buy stamps
there is a large, retarded girl
with filthy glasses.
                    Each time,
an impatient grandmother
must show her how to fold the page
to tear the stamps free.
Each time, concentrating stupidly,
the girl begins creasing it mid-stamp.
Scorn rolls from the old woman's
fishy mouth: "My God, what have you done?"
she might be saying. "No...
like this...at the perforations."
Tiny, cocoa hands puppeteer larger,
incapable fingers to remove a swatch of stamps
that will end up in trash bins in Illinois.

On the other hand,
I don't know her rapid tongue.
Could she instead be saying,
"Wretched girl, listen to that beautiful
music. Why can't *your* fingers do that?"

or

"This man's people bombed us,
so your mother is crippled, so you are slow."

In a land of bland perfection,
honey voices, and yellow tailored suits,
this girl is a clod
           but I remember her best—
like a mole on a lover. She is radiant.
She is Miss Japan.

The Peony

Blessed be the peony, vomited from its sepals,
Adjacent to the callow, craning bud, a green globe
On which the ants toil It will soon see
the sea of fluffy velveteen that composes its family,
That the sun favors so shamelessly,
That butterflies change directions in mid-butterflight to see
And light upon. If indeed the peonies were any brighter, blind
People would see them. They
Would gather and gaze, and the neighbors would say,
"Those are the blind, and it's the peonies they have congregated to behold."
Despite the efforts of the industrious anemones,
Roses, perfidious forsythia, and crocuses,
No thing outblooms, outshines the peonies
That line the driveway.

The peony is a home:
Once, an ant walked across its middle,
Hesitated in the middle's midst,
And thought, "Here I am, and there is where I must go"
Before walking to the other side.
A small grasshopper escaped a sparrow and hopped in the peony
And hid and waited in the shade of the petals
That conceal the stigma, the style (and the pedicel);
And the sun went down behind the garage
And cast a pink cast on the siding
That complemented the peonies which are pink and yellow and fat—
A child is being beaten in the house the peonies are at.

THE DAFFODIL

The daffodils watched the dinosaurs die on Christmas Eve
of the cosmic calendar.
These first flowers (jonquils, daffodils, or proto-daffodils)
waved indifferently, a horn section swinging mutely in the sooty air,
a silent requiem for Rex and Sue who coughed on meteor dust,
stumbling crazily, weak with hunger, falling.

See, long before there were people to think them up,
ideas were operating, and the idea had been that if you were
endowed with sharp enough fists to dethroat your neighbor
or swift enough legs to make off with her eggs,
you got to have another lunch, and that was good.
The daffodil stood for a new idea,
and that was, go ahead and be fragile,
but be beautiful and have a fierce sense of irony,
and be sweet enough to rope others into doing your bidding.
Enslave the bees of prehistory, have sex delivered
to your petals and serve a sugary potion there.

"Hello my name is Jeff Dahmer; I like the way you dance."

The daffodil's shape anticipates the old fashioned telephone earpiece,
simultaneously phallic and vulvic.
With its genitals defining its very form,
a flower's principal role is sex.
The other job of flowers has always been to watch funerals.
From its first triceratops to last week's obituary,
the daffodil has been there for death—
adorning the sickroom, the mass, and the tomb.

"You'll just die when I tell you this, but I'm in love with you already."

This duality mirrors that of the human libido:
One aspect wanting to (pro)create, the other to kill—

One noticing the curve of buttocks, the lips' portrayal of labia;
the other aroused by the tenderness of the neck's arteries,
the softness of the eyelid and its proximity to the brain.
One man anticipates taking his wife as he drives from the office;
Another can't wait to come home from the Ambrosia Chocolate Company
and dine on real ambrosia—oh yes, real ambrosia *has to* be flesh.

Gilles de Rais is forgiven, Sagawa is worshipped,
J. W. G. sits plump in his hospital painting scarlet hollyhocks,
while you suffered. *I* sent you that arrangement, Jeff,
(jonquils and wild pansies).

"I love you so completely, I'll suck the marrow from your bones"

See, in a better world you could love someone that completely;
you could cook and eat sixteen brown boys without shame
(and new ones would sprout up in their places like warts)
and you would be whisked away, not to a court of law,
but to a court of aesthetics, where the question would not be
"How could you?" but *"What did it taste like?"*

The Marigold

As the eyelash moon grazes the roof
of the bar where the actresses drink,
and the blue blink of the neon martini icon
eclipses her light,
a satin pump leads a leg over the bar stool:
You are safe for now, my love.

It is remarkable how the female genitalia
can resemble the lily.
It is remarkable: your milky skin and delicate neck
atop your die-in-childbirth frame—if I had a tail I would wag it.
Your eyes are dull and fearless on a night no other girl is out.
We drink to your boldness—you fitting the (victim) profile to a T
and the Disemboweler still at large.

Rumor has it he beat one victim with her own arm
torn out at the shoulder; yanked another's uterus out with his teeth.
I heard that he lay next to his victims afterwards
mimicking their broken bodies, sprawled out
like swastikas, their frozen expressions,   records of
losing one's soul
Can I interest you in a tangerine?
I met the farmer up in Bakersfield. He said,
one day God ate an orange and spit out the seeds.
The trees that grew bore tangerines.

You impart your past with less discretion with each gin and tonic.
I reveal nothing because I want to go back and kill who I was
and those who knew me then. An orgasm of the soul—
that must be how killing feels.
(Of course the key to killing is not to brag about it afterwards.)
But you wouldn't understand because you are green—
I had lived and died and been reborn and died and been reborn
when you were just the violence he would someday do to you in your

father's eyes.
You are a lily: slender, pale, and hollow.
I do not think I'm better than you; it's only a suspicion.
Your courage comes from ignorance, from liquor.
You pout and watch the dancers, an old cowboy and his lady,
so let's change the subject and dance that way
and rub and kiss and dance the way the lilies sway
as we hear the tortured voice of Miss Kitty Wells,
sweeter than the tangerine section in your mouth,
or even whole groves of tangerines,
or the tangerine (on the bar),
with its tangerine-colored color,
oranger than oranges, marigolds, or the flame of the soul.
Agriculture is violence. The soul is what's looking out your eyes

The Carpenter and the Moon

The Carpenter wastes there in the cool night,
hands that held many nails now held *by* nails.
His ears ring. You can tell by the moon
that it's almost Easter. A thief has died.

"For God so loved the world, that He sacrificed His only begotten Son..."
In other words, when you love somebody, kill it something
special. The moon observes this Child abuse
upon which a world is built and thinks,
"This reminds me of that thing with Abraham,
only this is *much* worse."

The Carpenter has descended to collect the good people of hell.
His mother weeps. The moon remarks,
"A good father *marries* your mother."
A toolbox is auctioned:
because when a carpenter dies, the world has an extra one.

The moon becomes jealous, remembering
when *she* was worshipped, not some Senseless Act.
She wanes to nothing, but she doesn't
blame the diet industry or glossy waifs from *Mirabella*—
she is just turning in her black bed
regular as a drum beat.

Apollo defines her fairly

yet she is saddled with lunacy, menstruation, and Monday.
Yes, she too is useless,
but there is a difference between gratuitous cruelty and gratuitous beauty.

Her aluminum glow adorns like a rosary
but warms no one.
She hasn't washed anyone's feet lately,

and she's done nothing for the people of hell,
who are: gamblers, fools, and dreamers,
suicides, different drummers, and wasted drummers
like Karen Carpenter and Keith Moon.

WHEN DOES A BRIDE WEAR BLACK?

When she is Christ's bride.
                        But anyway
not very long ago there was
a very rich woman who'd fired her maid
and had to prepare a dinner for thirteen
herself. She listened to the radio
as she basted the lamb. There had been
a terrible earthquake in Tokyo.
To her dismay she discovered
she was missing a salt spoon
and she began to weep. Soon
Christ appeared to her
with the tiny spoon in His
palm. "I scoured the pawn
shops," He said. "It is a miracle."
"Why," said the woman, "are you helping
me when thousands lay dead in Japan? I am
just a rich and silly woman."
Christ said, "You are rich because you are beautiful—
you glow with charm and intelligence.
You are devout and good.
You are the stars in my sky.
You are the ripples on the water I walk on.
You, the faithful.
We are each other's prisoner.
We couldn't be more intimate
if we jumped into a jet engine together."

Miracles take muscle.
Christ's eyes are constantly running back and forth
over the earth
                like the eyes of a poet—
the opium dream eyes of Walt Whitman
the black and piercing eyes of Emily Dickinson

the suave, rueful eyes of Baudelaire
the kind and canine eyes of Frost
Auden, with one angry eye, one frightened
eye, the birdlike eyes of John Ashbery
William Carlos Williams with the eyes of
birds of prey, Robert Creeley with a flap of elephant
flesh where an eye is missing, Blake's huge and wronged
and womanish eyes, Byron with those thundering eyes.

Thunder is Christ's applause
(His hands of special design:
holes to cut down on wind resistance).

He takes in the whole show:
a child's supermarket tantrum,
a homosexual struck from the list
of those who get to live,
two Jewish teenagers vomiting
after the break-fast of Yom Kippur,
an idiot child clapping while his father weeps.
Christ regrets he has but two eyes
to cry with,
   and in the Orient, where the riddle goes,
"What is the sound of one hand clapping,"
a hand inches out
from under a ruined pagoda.
     All are wanting.

There is a woodcut of conquistadors
chopping off the hands of Indians
resistant to conversion.
But what of the Zen master
who chopped off a student's finger
to make a point?

Eastern religion is false
(like a wolf wearing wool)
with its wise and gentle posturing:
its trickiness is really an act of aggression
against the healthy mind.
Dismembering children is unacceptable in any pedagogy.
Which is why I am a nun.
Zen is forbidden
here—a ruler on the knuckles
leaves the child intact
if bloody. The only Riddle in town is Christ
because clapping, *by definition,* takes two hands.

The Babysitter

And God
created woman,
and she was boyish
and tall, and she was
ignored when her lips were unlacquered
or her legs were unwaxed.

Eve talked to other bachelorettes, bled,
talked to her cat, looked in the mirror, smoked,
looked in the mirror, smoked, talked to herself,
but something
was missing:
something stocky and crass,
something that would smack her and then bring her flowers,
something that would smack her and then kiss her and bring her flowers.

"Yo. Wallflower."
"Yes, stocky one?"
and she knew,
yes then she knew
that this was her lunch ticket.

Time passed and
one day, Eve invented the colon:
She wrote:
>   There is a word for what I do:
>   I brood.

Eve wrote:
>   I dusted today. God came over. I washed the walls.
>   I sharpened the knife. I read a little. Oh, I have to
>   remember to buy mutton
> >   mutton
> >   bread

            cheese

            wax paper

I wonder if I'm getting enough iron. I really wonder
if I get enough.

And she wrote:

      The bastards are with the babysitter.

      I love them so.

      I love their father not.

      He is not very other-worldly

      but he is my lunch ticket and

      the lunch ticket of the children—

      I am no longer it.

      I am no longer

      boy crazy.

Eve forgot to make lunch.
She sang. She imagined other things
and she wrote:

      I imagine I have a lover.

      He is tall and pessimistic.

      He wears cotton things on his tall, pessimistic frame.

      He is bookish and we go out Dutch treat.

      I lick the stamps on the postcards he sends me.

      I lick the stamps and this is our kiss.

      This is our kiss and I love him with all my being.

      He is away now but he will return.

      I stick my finger in the proof that he will return

      and I taste the fruit

      and I roll in the proof that he will.

Eve changed and she wrote:

      Today I made apple pie.

      I must remember to make Medieval beef.

I wonder if I should poison some of the animals
that come in the garden.
I wonder if I should put poison on small pieces of food
and leave it out for the animals that come in the garden.
I feel like maybe taking the children's milk money
and buying a pair of those white stockings everybody's wearing.
Maybe then I would be happy.

Eve looked in the mirror
and she wrote:
        I am a heifer.
        Every day I become less attractive.
        I no longer bleed
        but there is a word for how I bruise.
        He spoke to me today.
        He said, "What can I give you?
        What can I give you
        never to sing again?"

Eve was no longer attractive or
prolific, she bruised "prolifically,"
and the guy, well, he
found someone younger:
we'll call her
"Jenny."

Redemption

I learned about Santa Claus, about Christ,
before I learned we were Jews
                        and about the oil that burned for eight days
instead of only one
                and heard how my mother
watched her sister beaten to death
by Irma Grese in Auschwitz.

The artificial Christmas
tree—with its felt stars of David—
dwarfed in every way the menorah
my mother told us came with them from Poland.

Though Jews, my parents exulted in Christmas.
There was something perverse
about their attention to every detail—
they wore the traditions of the goyim
like a garish Easter hat.
                        Once, my father told us he'd bribed Santa Claus
to overlook the rules and visit us.
                        My mother taught us hymns
and Bible verses she'd learned to fool the Nazis.

One night I dreamed that Christ
                        came down the chimney
instead of Santa Claus
and emerged from the fireplace, sweaty, His hands
caked with blood (He'd killed Santa).
He leered at me and said, "The charade is over,
Jewboy."
        I was attracted.

                Now,
also in my thirty-third year,
                and dying,

I feel closer than ever to Him.
                    I have converted.
My stigmata appear in livid lesions on my hands and face,
plum blue, the hue of ink used to stamp
the expiration day on meat.
I read one of the Gospels and ask,
"Is this God's punishment?"
The priest says, "No, that's what hell is for."

It's the coldest Christmas on record.
The dogs are curled up
in front of the hearth like cocktail shrimp.
In the woods you hear the false gunshots
of sap freezing and cracking.
The air itself freezes
and clatters to the ground
like a lie.
If you bother to look,
everything is clearer
as if cut out with sharp scissors,
and you see, as if seeing
through a new pair of glasses,
you see the truth for the first time:

                My parents did leave Europe in a hurry,
                        but no Jew smuggles a menorah
                    into a death camp and what's more,
                            comes out holding it.
            It is the kind of thing that got left behind,
                            with everything
        when the soldiers' boots pounded on the stairway.
                One took only the clothes on his back
                        and perhaps a photograph
                    to throw from the train window
                        to say, "I was here."

My parents were like the soldiers.
Like mistletoe
strangling an elm,
they occupied the home
of disappeared and wealthy Jews,
and when they came to America as "Jewish refugees,"
the stolen menorah was their story, their passport.

This is admitted
with an honesty reserved for those
baptized nightly by night-sweats.
My flesh sucked into a teetering frame
sparks their memories of Auschwitz.

There is a monster in the mirror.
My eyelashes fall out.
The lines on my face are
an elegy for enthusiasm.
The latest pill doesn't work.
I read the Gospels and ask,
"Is this all there is?"
The priest says:
> "It may seem that the teachings of Our Lord
> are somewhat commonplace, devoid of profundity —
> 'be nice,' 'don't sell stuff in church,'
> and so on… But that simply isn't the point:
> if we liked Jesus because He was witty, original,
> that would be decadent.
> One must have faith —
> especially now that no one will kill us if we don't."

They say that to love others
you have to love yourself.
This is a non sequitur.
Self-hatred is underrated.

The most liberating feeling in the world
is to let go of all sympathy for oneself.
You must look at yourself
as you would a neighbor's silly child.
This is where Redemption begins.
This is where you go beyond shame—
you feel the looks of horror in the video store,
the fatigue, the weeping sores, and you feel
this is what being Christ is *like*,
His fey aura clings like a soaking blanket. Oh,

and I saw my murderer today
at the newsstand. His tiny
obituary caught my eye
like a brightly-wrapped present.

Contrary to the greeting card,
the message is not about forgiveness

                              but accepting Mystery.
This Christmas,
with all the adoration for the Holy Infant the season inspires,

we must remember to feel a little bit of hate

                                  for His killers
and those who just stood there.

FLICKER

These new holidays,
Martin Luther King Jr. Day, Earth Day—who needs them?
Integration is a failure, the Dream is a charred carcass,
and the earth is overrated.

We need a holiday called "Flicker"
so named because on this day
stoplights blink from red to green
with a rapid, irregular rhythm
causing car crashes.
Flicker is a celebration of menopause hot flashes,
a reflection on genocide, a Halloween of behaviors,
a time of confusion, perversity, turning inward,
a nod to the fragility of stability, the fickleness of physics.
Flicker is on April 20.
On Flicker, a woman might set fire to her sleeping man.
Each Flicker, children set fire to men who are asleep on trains.
On Flicker, feel panic go all through you:
You Are Alone,
                    and no one—not Lassie, not even Flipper—can save you.
Christmas has *It's a Wonderful Life*,
Easter has *The Greatest Story Ever Told*,
and Flicker has the Zapruder footage of the Kennedy assassination;
and at that frame when the top off his head flies off,
you can't help but think of Emily Dickinson.
"Domenique-Nique-Nique-Nique," the singing nun sang that week—
boy was her life sad.
On Flicker in 1889, Hitler debuted from the womb.
He cried and cried,
taking huge quotas of air between each noisy exhalation
of fear and discomfort.
Frau Hitler held him when he was finally out of danger.
He was soft. She was joyous.
All those miscarriages.

So many tears.
She gazed into his face thinking, "I should name him 'Mirakel'," and
"When does the soul enter the body?"
Is it, to paraphrase one heretical poetess, still pouring
in through the fontanelle up to the moment it slams shut?
This theory has profound implications vis-à-vis the abortion debate:
One could legally throw infants out windows, do in a harelipped toddler.
Or is the soul intact at conception?
Well, does a match light as soon as you strike it?

No, it does not. There is that split second
where the match whispers "church!
Inhales
           and is alight.
That moment is Flicker,
when you can kill.

THE FARM

And there you are, the last pin-up, in your stockings and fur coat,
your pale face gorgeous with mischief, tarty. You were December.
Remember the farm, in December?
A junked car hood for a sled, being yanked through
the dead white field behind the pick-up,
the iced air summoning blood to our cheeks...
I associate you with velocity:
your skiing, your lead foot
(taking out a mailbox while fixing your lipstick),
the way you piled a lifetime into 23 years.
As stunning as you were, you didn't make a pretty corpse:
the windshield bruise, the draining coma,
they did your hair wrong, the dress was frowzy,
and worst of all, Natalie, they farmed you—
plucking organs from you before you were cold.
A letter they sent your mother lists
what they used and couldn't use, what part went to whom
in what neighboring town.
Economics pollutes everything.
The haggling with the funeral home.
That soloist who couldn't sing beautifully.
A bogus diamond on your earlobe,
fodder for the coffin robber at the wake,
a boyfriend.

And now, in this new December,
A vision haunts me:
Your mother wanders some hardware store
(a chandelier fell, she needs some wire)
when she spots a stranger, and although he is wholly unremarkable,
she is attracted, filled with ache.
She follows him, forgetting her shopping
She heads him off in automotive
and stares—he looks back dully—until it hits her:
You have my daughter's eyes

The Body Burners

The doms hoist onto the pyre the body
bundled in cloth, a fat merchant who in life they never could have
touched. They are untouchables,
people who are said to grieve
when a child is born
and celebrate when one dies.

You may not believe it,
but it is said we live in the time of Kali,
the goddess of destruction,
the one with green skin and a skirt of human arms.
You see her on cigarette packages,
on buses, she is beloved
in Varanasi, like this minute's calendar girl.

Varanasi, the holiest city,
is lit gold in the morning;
the sun reflects off the flood plane sands
white as butter
on the far bank of the Ganges.
Close to river, under the watch of the temples,
the doms burn bodies around the clock
like mortician Sisyphuses. The fire,
older than Christ and as sacred,
is kept blazing by death.
A dom lights a new one with sticks
from another. Another dom
tongs legs back over a pyre
which has consumed everything else,
He does it with the flair of a ham actor.
Fat drips and spatters.
Mourners are tearless.
They glower at you or chatter or smoke pot
or just watch.

Kali's tongue hangs from her mouth
in anticipation of drinking the blood of everyone

                                    when she has lain everything to waste.
                                              Even motion will cease.
                                                   But that is good,
                                          because Vishnu can go to sleep,
                                                 and when he wakes
                                        it will start again, a new "day."

Ten or more corpses are burning
at any hour on discreet mounds of wood.
It smells like the meal
of a bad cook.
Widows used to commit suttee;
Now they chain smoke.
People are bathing in the filth of the Ganges
into which the ashes are raked.
Boats of wood pull up and park.
There is no silence:
Crackle, crackle,
dogs fight over a finger,
wood is stacked, hiss,
footsteps.

                    Kali used to have flesh, her demon blood coursed through it,
                                              impulses roiled in her.
                                           Now she is only an image...

                                  But that is the age of Kali for you.
                                          The world is already dying.
                            Things lose their bodies, their creature-ness.
                                        Everything becomes metaphor.
                                                 Things do not exist,
                                                        but mean.
                                                 No one believes
                                                      in belief.

Like a loud champagne cork
the merchant's skull pops when its

contents boil, gases blow out the back of the head.
It is the climax,
it is the moment
the soul is released from its prison.
Mourners disperse
and cannot look back.
A centipede crawls over your foot.
Your body is a church of nerves.
The breath on the back of your neck
is not Christ's.
              India changes your life:
You have so much to learn.

THE DAY'S EYE

My knee is not a flower,
Bee. On this deck, five floors
Up, miles from any meadow,
How is it that you are plump?
Do you suck
The soda pop from the sidewalk?
Did you notice the broken heart
Shape box spilling from the trash
And taste a discarded creme?
Or visit a cut daisy at the Korean
Market? Dead like that,
Is the nectar as sweet?
Is there nectar?

I saw you on a pigeon carcass on Attorney Street—
                                        is there nectar there?
Do you know?

The guilt of drowning a bee as a child
        stung long after the swollen bite had healed,

And that was because I could see

The delicate legs patting the side of the pail

Trying to escape something so slippery

        Plastering my wound,
        Grandma stiffened
        When I sought to dry
        My tears in her apron.
        "Saints come back as bees
        And sting sinners," she said.

Bouncing up to my head
Stinger poised, do you smell

My memories of killing?
When you explore a shirt
Button, do you see my heart?
Is my heart black?
When you buzz and hover,
Does the soul pour out the skin
For inspection? Far from the hive
In this baked and flowerless
Landscape, are you St. Joan
On her pyre longing for a
Drink? Here among the clouds
Are you St. Peter
Examining me from scarred
Knee to shampooed hair?
Who are you?
And what have I done?

OCCUPIED PARIS, 1994

A mother explains to her child
That when the exterminator comes that afternoon
Even his favorite beetle cannot be spared.
"We cannot differentiate between insects in cages
And those that get into the onions," she says.
The subsequent regard from her child
Nearly breaks her heart.

"Let me
Put it this way: Every German officer
Had a favorite Jew—a 'good' Jew
—But each one understood
That none, not one Jew, could be spared."
The child seems to understand
And the mother holds the child's hand as he opens
The cage and caves the beetle's head in with his thumb.
They stand there then, gazing out the sunny window
Onto to the cracked pavement of rue Goebbels
The child's face against his mother's thigh
Her hand in his black hair until the exterminator's
Knock is heard.

        It is the tenderness
Of moments like these, that nothing,
Not even history, can change.

Indian Summer

A mother calls for her son another time.
It is the time before the time before the time to begin worrying.
There was that time he'd been playing at the swamp late she'd worried
And on Halloween only days ago when she'd sent him out as Death,
His first year unescorted, he stayed out an extra hour enjoying himself so;
But on this beautiful and very warm day in November
When everything is dead but the whole world seems to be grinning,
Her call contributes pleasingly to the neighborhood's evening opera
Of calls of children's names and "dinner!" and "come home!".

Come inside, my precious beautiful one, she thinks in the spotless kitchen
Where the meat loaf is baked and though her husband is out of town
There sits a chilled pitcher of martinis. Her skirt rustles with a comforting
Authority as she charm-school walks to the door to which a knock has
Beckoned her. Her heart quickens in anticipation of her sweet blond boy
As she (her whole life has been a masquerade it turns out) opens the door
To reveal a policeman holding her son's ripped shirt. They look
At each other and there is that moment—that sick moment
Before everything is understood

Park Avenue, February 14

Snow banks are melting
leaving a skeleton of filthy lace.
I can hear the rush of the sewers
through ermine ear muffs. The city
is ugly with the last bloody coughs
of winter, but I am happy.
Now I'm sad. Now I'm happy.
In my short suede skirt I imagine
I'm a flower in the sludge.
In my slick eel skin heels
I am happy to have animals die for me—
it makes me feel like a Hungarian countess
with subjects. Now I'm falling (help),
but at once
         a man I hadn't seen
has me firmly by the shoulders
I look up,
         happy that I'm a woman
and that he is a man.

The Wind

The wind (and not the baby) sprang up at 4 A.M.
and woke Cousin Nancy
and whispered of mortality among the nightingales
She looked then in the mirror at eyes that last she saw in tears
and sat and spent the morning mourning at the window,
watching the nightingales as their flight revealed the wind,
which, though unseeable, contained, she ascertained, the spirit of death.

Beside the sill lay *The Boston Evening Transcript*
with the headline "PRIEST DROWNS BABY IN BAPTISM".
Her child was no death by water but was claimed by wind-fanned flames
She hadn't even named him before he'd fallen kill.
What do you call something that is born and then dies in April?

She was a hollow woman. He'd gone
without a bang a whimper or a gurgle.

She looked then at the cat,
the pitch-blackened bassinet, the TV set blaring sportsspeech,
and the bisque porcelain children (and such kitsch) on the bureau;
and she thought she'd eat a peach
and name the baby T.S. — after her hero,
Tom Seaver. Boy, was he a pleasure to watch pitch.

NATALIE

Why should this lesson be at your expense?
The loss is big,
And graceless—

> it can't be so,
> it can't be so,

As if my heart has been twisted backwards in my body—

> it *is* so.

I'm confused.
My head is the clapper.
The sides of the bell are the knowledge.
The bell tolls, and it hurts, and it *is* so, and the hearts
Twisted backwards there in our bodies, and our
Hands squeeze at our sides as we sing at the dull church service,
And we sing, but our heads bang against that hard, cold metal—

> *we* need her,
> *we* need her—

God, what makes You think You need her more?
For You, Asshole, have eternity.
Our lives are the time it takes You to spit.

> Natalie, I dreamed I walked with you
> and you were strong.
>
> Last week I spoke to you
> on the phone.
>
> I have a picture of you in Hawaii.
> You were laughing.
>
> How can we honor you?
> Spray-paint your name on every Toyota?
> Contribute to your stoic mother's Sad Book?
> Begin stitching the car crash quilt?

There is a tribe in North America that divvies up
The possessions of their dead. I carry books in your black
Tennis bag bearing the brand name "Head".
I want something else.
I know what it is.

It's clear now —
            As clear as the windshield that was your exit:
            I'll take your unapologetic smirk.
            I'll put it on right now.
            There.
            Now. Just one question:

How can we heal when your memory follows every brunette?

STALK

Even her footsteps were sexy.
Still, it was clear she was seeing another man:
the disappearing, returning exhausted and empty-handed
after day-long shopping sprees, the telephone call she thought I didn't hear.
"No, nobody knows. I love you. Good-bye."
I followed her to his house
                              and waited.
I barged in.
She was rocking him in her arms.
It was her brother Bob, dying.
She looked at me.
"It was a secret," she wept.

She rode with him on his roller coaster of health.
She brought him pills for each new infection,
but AIDS thinks of everything.
I had met him
blushing, strapping.
Now he'd vomited blood on her.
What a cruel June, July and August
without even a lemonade's worth of happiness.
My black and cloven heart.
I have no faith—
I even look at my fingers when I type.
I am shamed by the wanton compassion of others.
The Italian nuns who went to the hospital in Kikwit to care for the sick
knowing they too would die
horribly.
The river is swollen with corpses.
Even the worst parts of hell are more luxurious.

Death is like that:
always the same, always different.
You can almost hear in the rush of the falls,
"give up poetry, give up poetry..."

THE HOUSE OF CARDS

Have you ever followed a beautiful woman?
The one who wore no nylons,
tapped her foot to an interior tune,
and blew on her soup
                              just for you,
whose thick black hair bounced on her sweater
as she left the café everyday
to freshen the street with her wrap-around skirt. Oh
where do beautiful women go?

Do they return to where they are kept in a stack?
Do they have jobs as visions in dreams?
Does desire steer them to me?
                              No.
She holds her book to her breast and walks
several blocks to the nursing home
on the south side of town.
She signs in and goes to a room
and takes *The History of Civilization* from her bosom
and balances it on the gate,
the gate in the door frame,
like the kind for a dog,
that keeps in a skeletal girl—
legs splayed like blades in a Swiss Army knife—
who sits in a puddle
and clutches in oversized knuckles
a doll whose facial buttons she's bitten off.
Her skirt's filled with diaper.
Her teeth are ground flat.
Her spine is curved
like a carnival mirror.
From her lip goes a delicate string
to the chewed food on her breasts.
She doesn't look up but scoots to the gate.
Despite her gnarled body and her IQ

(lower than the number of cards in a deck)
make no mistake—you can see
by her elegant neck,
by that wavy black hair down her back—

                             they are twins

(life is so unfair).

Grunts come—she cannot form words—her twisted arms
contort to the two signs she knows:
                        "Hug"
                            "Please"
Civilization will topple like an infant giraffe
succumbing to anthrax.

The Waltz

When had she felt this way before?
There was that time a window fell on her hand
and all she could see was her surprise in the glass because it was dark
outside.

She liked the format:
the streets offered HAMBURGERS PIZZA GIRLS GIRLS GIRLS and more
and there was more love because there was more people
and that night she dreamed about a vineyard sliding down a rocky cliff
into the sea.

He bought her a grape Crush for starters
and she liked him more than Christmas.
He gave her a drug that made her not from Nebraska
and made whiskers on his face
swirl like clouds.
He kissed her too, because he was an artist
and he left her with reminders
like the morning map to the bus station he drew on a napkin
and the hardened snot on her panties wasn't snot

and on the bus she closed her eyes again
and the grapes that broke on the rocks had the sweetest juice
but it was juice nevertheless.

A Note on the Refrigerator

The fruit drawer is empty.
The ham is in its tub.
Don't look in the butter dish.
Tonight let's talk about what you did.
That's aspic in the gravy boat—
don't do what I did, expecting something sweet.
All in all, it's a pretty good refrigerator full—
those beets are old and the pearl onions peaked,
but that cauliflower, and Christ, those watercress sandwiches
from the shower, the juice, the soup, the spoo...
If that ham were a steak I'd put it on my wound.
Not that I'm mad about it at all
because we're all human
and when we do things like borrow someone's soap
or eat someone's plums or mislay a skate
key, it's not that we're selfish or inconsiderate or anything bad.
It's just that we are aardvarks,
sucking up ants like there's no tomorrow.

Possess-possess

I give you 7:39 p.m.,
I give you peonies, peas, me—

Shut up, *I'm* saying a poem,
but it isn't about a sunset, you, or a garden,
Those things I grind my cigarette out on,
the world is my grapefruit, I don't stop for cars.

I love you, you're my army, my grapes,
you're my syringe—

What? (Yawn), this is my song: my gun, my wine, my heroin
are for me, I have what is my oyster by the hair. I am.
Complete—so you are
a parasite—I'm more sans you, 30% more.

Then: I am your mistletoe, your insect, your toothbrush,
your suitcase, I know.

Wait, I'm saying something,
my golf course, my coffee, my guitar, my finger
need no mower, no sugar, no strings, no ring.
I came in your store, didn't find what I wanted, excuse me I belched.

My shop has a turnstile, a lock, wet paint, a policy:
You Break Something You Pay.

Ha, I see, but this is my story, my
breakfast, my park bench, my river: you're not my cocoon,
nor my trampoline nor my spittoon, nor my soap with which I wash—

You listen, you, I am your green tea, your cloak, your sash,
I am your river, that which is my oyster is you—

May I tell you this, what you think is yours is actually —

   and furthermore I'm your plug-in, your bottle, your blinker,
   your keyboard, your door, your pistol, your pestle, your nest,
   your Blistex, your shower, your mirror, your wafer,
   your bright florid Doris Day day.

Niagara Falls

A poet can't change the world
but he can ruin your evening.
No wonder poets are paid less
than the homeless:
they annoy you longer.
On the other hand, a painter *can* change the world:
look at Hitler.
I am painting my apartment in May.
It's a beautiful spring day in the State of New York.
It sounds like a conceit,
but I dream in poetry.
I dreamed I was dancing on a hillside and singing,

> "It's a beautiful day,
> and Doris Day is in town.
> Let's grab a lemonade
> and hit the fairground.
> Let's kiss a butterfly
> and kill twenty-four hours.
>
> Leave Grandma in the car
> and hold hands and kill a child.
> We'll kill a butterfly
> and kiss twenty-four hours.
> It's a gorgeous afternoon
> and Susan George is here to stay."

I am bursting with joy!
And the reason is:
money: the State of New York gave me some money.
Let's rename New York, New Yellow
for its tremendous sunshine.
Even if I am hit by a bus,
I will be shipped to Paradise!

(the town in California where my parents live)
I would kiss Mussolini if he gave me $7000.
Did you hear we're going to Italy,
my money and me?
I so love this world,
this better mousetrap world,
a world where Money and Joy are twins
at a fork in the road,
a world I am changing in tiny, tiny ways.
I shop and shop!
I kiss Voltaire!
i love the state of New York!
Did you hear the good news?
Christ, Jesus is coming   and
Icarus didn't fall for the reason you think: he was shot.

Quince

My students see history as a single
moment they call "back then"
like a flash of tinsel turning
on the Christmas tree in an unfelt air current.

We overlook how modern
medieval and Renaissance painters were—
Take Robert Campin's *Annunciation*
with Mary in a little Dutch house,
unwimpled, not even glancing up from her book—
Joseph is in the next room building
mousetraps. Everything is brand
spanking up-to-date circa 1425: Mary's gold-brocaded
red dress pouring like blood toward the angel,
oak and walnut furniture with dog and lion finials,
and Mr. And Mrs. Ingelbrecht at the door, spying in.
It's like a twentieth-century painter putting
the Virgin in Capri pants and Italian sunglasses
(angels come to you with a great
deal of light) while Joseph restrings
a tennis racket with new cat gut.

But that's how it is also with
God, for Whom everything that's ever
happened and will ever happen happens
all at once.
                Shakespeare pens the final
line of *Othello*— "*This heavy act with
heavy heart relate*"—as O. J. Simpson
vows to stop at nothing to find the killer
of the ex-
wife he's killing.
In a nano-second barbed wire is invented, used,
and reinvented: today the barbs are longer,

flatter, and stainless as a kitchen.
Jenny and I look at the unicorns and Campin's
triptych hanging in the Cloisters
in the same instant that the last brush strokes dry on
it and everything else that ever got
a fresh coat of paint,
                         like the door
on the third floor of the Humanities building—
when I went to class this morning it had "hittler"
scrawled on it in black supermarket magic marker.
The swastika that accompanied it was comically
wrong, the hooks backwards,
facing each other.
                    After class it was history,
red enamel concealing, hardening.

And just as the earth, with all its mountains and abysses,
would be smoother than the smoothest billiard ball
were it shrunk to that size,
                         so too do human events
flatten out before God—
Jenny selecting a mineral
water at the bodega and Sophie's choice
loom with equal significance or insignificance
while polar ice caps melt in the time of Exodus.

When You're God, eternity is already over,
but at the Cloisters, Jenny gives me
a quince she plucked from a tree in the courtyard,
her eyes like eightballs, eyes
that could heat Russia, shining
with the mischief of every woman
who ever offered
a boy fruit...

Man's Fate

One day Ernest Hemingway was writing a novel in which there was much struggle and a great deal of blood. Suddenly he found himself at a point in the plot where there were three women in a room full of children. He paused, furrowing his brow. He continued after consideration and had the women pass out snacks which the children ate up hungrily. When there was no more food left, Hemingway paused again, stuck. He realized that the women must now have a discussion of solemn importance amongst each other and amongst the children. The unique wisdom of the women and the children was to be the key to the struggle, but, for one thing, they spoke an odd language Hemingway could not place. He sputtered. He realized he was out of his element. He paced and rubbed his neck, which was red and thick. He stomped and cursed and flung something.

> His despair increased:
> he fell to his knees
> and gnashed his teeth.
> He tore at his clothing
> Moaning and sobbing.
> Finally he began to wail and
> flop about prostrate like
> an immense marlin.
>
> After he had spent well over an hour
> of weeping and heaving like this
> an angel of Nordic beauty
> appeared to disturb his agony.
> She whispered sweetly unto him,
> she whispered unsweetly to him,
> she sweetly unwhispered to him,
> she whispered sweetly to un him,
> "You must change your life, see?
> You, the one cock of the walk."

Defeated, exhausted, and aware
of his obsolescence, Hemingway

trod back to his desk, dis-shod,
disposed of the unfinished manuscript
rubbed his eyes, removed a shotgun
from the cabinet, and

This is one theory.

RESPONSE

If nice guys finish last,
Long live failure.

Deconstruction

The new Pope elected yesterday
Is not only the youngest in history
But he is unusual looking
And hooked up on life support. He cannot wear the ring.

Or the hat in his delicate position
But he remarked, "I am not a monster."
He is the talk of Phillipsburg, Montana
His home town, where supporters and others gather outside the diner.

To catch a glimpse of Pope John-John and chatter.
One says, "Is it true he may die?"
"Nothing is black and white," is the reply.

Two factions comprise the crowd
That occupies the interior of the diner:
One is the Billings chapter of N.O.W.,
The other is a church group up from Salmon.

The focus is the red-haired waitress
Who sits perched atop the refrigerator
Threatening to jump.
     A hush blankets the prattle.

As a slow murmur, then a respiratory rattle,
And then a small small voice crescendoes ever so
Faintly from the vicinity of the waitress's swollen middle.
A woman adorned with tiny feet earrings

Cries out, "Bless me, your swallowed-wholeness!"
But she is subdued so that the new Pope can be heard:
"Johnny johnny johnny johnny woops! Johnny
Woops! Johnny johnny johnny johnny."

The waitress is the first to speak—
She addresses her apron—"I'm sick
Of hearing about your ten fingers
And your ten toes—this is *my life*."

Comes the voice, "But Mommy—"
She: "Don't Mommy' me"
It: Don't Medea me!"
She: "Parasite!"
It: "Assasin!"

"A woman's autonomy rests on her right
To rule her own body," remarks Mrs. Knight.

"Pro-life!" from the rabble comes the counter-cry.
Mrs. Knight stands and speaks,
"Pro-life" is a fallacy, a sugar-coated term backing an ideology designed
        to marginalize and oppress women by usurping
        the dominion of their own bodies. It is an insidious
        conspiracy patented by patriarchal institutions—the church,
        the state, the family—for the sole purpose of enslaving
        women and, by proxy, denying their existence."
"Pro-choice!" is shouted in agreement.

The new Pope musters strength and replies:
"Pro-choice" is a fallacy. Our so-called "choices" are constructs of various
        discourses. In this case, I see two operating: on the one hand,
        the voice of tradition admonishes and shames women
        who have children out of wedlock, and on the other hand,
        bourgeois feminists, who seek to occupy positions within
        patriarchy rather than strive to dismantle it, devalorize child-
        rearing altogether in favor of careerism, and, with a
        dismissiveness that rivals that of the oppressor, adopt a
        discourse in which the life of the

unborn child is denied or
　　　marginalized out of existence. We live in a society that hates
　　　children, and, if those children happen to be sub-individuals
　　　like me, permits their slaughter.
　　　　　　　　　　　　　　Child-rearing,
　　　Ironically, is wherein lies women's greatest power. As the
　　　Primary source of nurture of the entire future populations, women
　　　Alone—armed with subversive discourses—own the recipe for
　　　Revolution."
The waitress, now in tears, is showing signs of backing down.
"The devil will always be convincing," Mrs. Knight warns her with a frown.
The waitress looks around the room and past the blur of faces
To a crow with a piece of straw in its beak flying past the diner,
As "Beware of false prophets," replies the new Pope, speaking ex-vagina.

The Last Supper

Actually, being middle easterners
it's likely they ate falafels.
But not all the myths are false.

People like to point out that because
Jesus was a middle-easterner and a Jew,
it is certain that he had jet-black hair, penetrating mahogany eyes,
and a dark, golden complexion—this just plain isn't true.

Part of the point of being Jesus is that you're different.
Trust the art. His hair was chestnut. His eyes were blue.
His skin was fair. (With that hot desert sun,
you can bet that's why the whores were always rubbing on ointment.)
This is one of the reasons why people were interested in him—
he looked exotic.

Jesus was thin.

During the meal,
a flood of thoughts and images
are darting about in the mind
of our savior like brightly-colored fish.

He was upset by a number of pertinent contradictions in his story.
He was hurt by the ostracism he had been subjected to by his people.
He felt ambivalence vis-à-vis the people around him.
He imagined someday coming back as a wallpaper hanger with a funny little
mustache and turning a whole bunch of them into, say, soap.
(But only if he became terribly bored and wicked.)
He wanted to write, but he didn't have a pen.

The people around him started chanting something
The falafel was bland, it needed something.
Bored, he looked at his wrist—one of his watches said midnight.
They sounded mundane. Bitter tahini. Which watch?

Poem

There was something African about the wallpaper in your eyes that night,
That night under the noisy squares,
You sang plaid holes and whispered disease in my dessert.

They say French pastry burned down the night you frightened the
furniture away,
They say the desks and chairs screamed Louise,
And your hair cemented circles around the blankets.

And the blankets shot loneliness at the foyer,
And later on we telephoned God's Niece Patty,
But Her light only dipped china in the blancmange,
Or the blancmange told us chin-ups tasted ghosts here.

Here is where cross scarves smear France on the curtains,
Here is my sandwich, the answer to cigarettes,
Climbing out the coat hanger of life,
My life is a piece of chalk in your bra,
And your bra is the key…to everything.

I love you,
You're my dog, my dog of love,
You press all the match sticks into the toast of solitude,
And sacrifice the gum of the world for the poor's coffin.

Haikus for my wife

Sweet pour, jacket my
throat—this kiss in the smoky
room with no windows.

Attack brown, false muse—
I only ask you to give me
courage, then sleep.

Down the hatch, slippery bride.
Embrace me from inside,
Kentucky temptress.

DIONYSIAN BREW

There is a sickness afterwards
To the body like a liquor grave

But worst of all is the sense
Of bewilderment
                    As if some mad, beautiful
Lover—the best you've ever had—has withdrawn
And run off
                    And as s/he goes, you realize—
That striped tail, those gold scales—s/he isn't even human
And s/he must return home
A place it takes lifetimes to get to.

And in knowing this
The sky darkens
                    Only a little

The Toy by Kate

I said this beer is so warm you could something an egg on it.
He and I broke up broke up because because he's rude and he doesn't like my haircut haircut.
I said Ed, make me beautiful.
He and I broke up broke up because because he's too selfish selfish.
I said listen, get your head out of the way of the television.
He and I broke up broke up because because he doesn't know how to conjugate the verb to share to share.
I said somebody called me imperious, Miss, get me a dictionary now!
He and I broke up broke up because because he's solipsistic and doesn't give a damn about others others.
I said *you* clean the apartment, *I'm* an artist.
He and I broke up broke up because because I need a rest and he's anal retentive retentive.
I said *you* feel cloistered, *you* need to find *your*self!
He and I broke up broke up because because he couldn't live with me ha! Me.
I said you toyed with my body, you toyed with my mind, you toyed with my *heart*, what am I?
He and I broke up broke up because because I made his mother cry cry.
I said ha! Tell me another one.
He and I broke up broke up because because I made him feel inferior inferior sexually.
I said cut the crap we both know what that hunk of plastic is for.
He and I broke up broke up because because he's a lousy cook and he's jealous of my career career.
I said don't talk to me that way, I have a small role in a new major film.
He and I broke up broke up because because of something I said I said.
I said you're just a little boy, here's your walking papers.
I said you're just a little boy, here's your walking papers.

THE SINKING

I found my sunglasses in a strange place this morning
I brushed my hair and took my sunglasses out of the sink
and put them on a chair.
I looked in a mirror and I pulled on my cheeks and looked at the pink
under my eyeballs.
I moved my sunglasses off the chair and picked up a plate.
I licked my thumb and rubbed a small yellow speck on the plate.
I put my sunglasses on the counter and opened the refrigerator.
I sat down in the chair.
I got up and shut the refrigerator and took my sunglasses off the counter
and walked over to my bed and laid them there.
I walked back to the counter and picked up a knife and put it in the sink
and walked back to the bed and picked up my sunglasses and walked back
to the counter and put them down and walked to the sink and turned on
the water.
I opened a drawer.
I opened another drawer.
I opened a third drawer.
I opened another drawer and a cupboard.
I plugged the sink.
I turned off the water.
I sat down in the chair and then got up and walked over to the bed and sat
down there and looked out the window and went back to the counter and
shut a drawer and picked up my sunglasses and put them on top of my
refrigerator.
I twisted the faucet harder.
There was a leak.
I looked at my sunglasses.
There were specks on my sunglasses, and there were specks floating in
the water.
There was this dead body in my apartment.
I went to one of the drawers and got out a towel and walked over to the
sink and dipped the towel in the water and wiped its face.
Wiped hard.

The water was hot.

The water was hot and the specks floated in it and the knife did not.

Metal doesn't float.

Falling new rockets have reminded us.

The Challenger is now a fish house.

Momma fish swims in this hole here and out that hole there.

Baby fish swims in that hole over there and swims over to some wires
and kisses a wire two times and swims over to a bone
and kisses the bone too.

The bone is Christa McCullough's, and one reads this in the paper and picks up a sweet roll and takes a bite and puts it back on the plate and turns it around.

THE AFFIRMATION

Listen. Is it laughter coming through the foggy dawn?
Yes, yeah, uh-huh, yes, yes. That would be you
they are laughing at. Fool.
With your chocolate streaks and the one eye you can't control,
the eye that creeps, creeps this way as the other
scans girls' stockings, the pigeons at their feet, and
their feet shod in patent leather,
that eye, stuck on the sky when you eat soup,
always too moist and crusted with God knows what
underneath. Curse you and your brace,
that brace that cash register clangs when you walk—no hobble. Scoot.
Yes, yes,
turn and look. Of course, why not, a dog barked.
That's it, marvel at this wonder of nature.
One of your friends, no doubt. Idiot! He's growling
and you clap, It, Thing. Look, look. Watch
where you tread. I can't afford to pay for any more
flowers. Not one forget-me-not, Son.

Yes, yeah, yes mm-hmm, yes. I know you're sorry.
Chin up. Watch the pebbles.
Are these pebbles cast at us? Of course. Affirmative.
Hoodlums. Get up, now, Coward! Don't cower. Be Spartan.
I look at you, and I look at failure.
You are a failure.
You should sign up—be the mascot—
for the Institute for the Promotion of Failure.
Yes, you with the grin and lint dangling from that curl.
You've crushed the back of your shoe.

Today, at church, I want you to picture Mother.
She loved you, Boy, with your favorite hat,
that freak eye, the medicines, and those
giant hands you don't keep out of things.

Look here, no television—I mean it—
no television if you rock and spit in the pew.
I can see the belfry.

I look at you with that brace, crooked mouth,
lumpy face, and I want to kiss you.
Though we are both men, I want to kiss you
on your mouth, packed with drool,
drool you wipe on your sleeve,
that sleeve, that sleeve on which you never wore your heart.

APARTMENT 4A

My war in the dark with my thoughts,
my genitals, my wife,
my cerebellum, my cigarette
lights up my face, burns my knuckles,
my life, my bed,
my wife, my thoughts, my darkness.

He stammers, he st
he's trouble-bled, he feigns function,
rationale, taste,
stabs darkness.

Cab waits, she cries chaos, cries on her eggs,
tries on a hat, tries on some glasses that
don't hide what her mouth, her forehead, her tissues show.

He has choices, has knowledge,
no life, no emotion, no motivation,
he lies face down on the pavement,
not drunk, not drugged, not dead.

Our bed, our neighbors, our candles
scream pain, scream light,
scream People want to sleep, it's 4 a. m.

It's 4A!

People cross out boxes, cross us, are cross,
throw water, push people, call names,
call help.

Policemen, firemen come, screech, park, shout,
make crumpled union with taxi, blink, panic, stir astonishment.

Doors open with interest, with fear,
with voluminous slippers, with small children,
4B, 4C, 4D, 4E,
forty of them cough smoke, scoff, cough disgust, discuss nonsense, blink tears,
shout fire, foray 4A.

Firemen focus frying pan, focus candle-holder, ashtray,
focus us, my wife, me, my God, my face
increases creases, decreases screaming,
twisting.

Theresa, Alex, Mrs. Roy, and the Klaussens clutch possessions,
their stomachs, squint up, look cold, try explanations,
try to be heroes, try his crime.

His war with the dark, his thoughts, his wife
cries breakfast, spills oil, cries we're through,
candles cry wax on newspapers about his problem
burning children, sale prices, shark attacks,
she throws hats, throws coats, glasses, anger in boxes
at the cab, the neighbors, his wife, the cops, the firemen,
for a return of composure, his wife
he she I we they wait.

I, I, I, I, yes I live in 4A
in darkness, in madness,
out of innocence, out of necessity,
out of water outside
they they they're
laughing at me, at my wife, at fire,
at 4A 4A 4A.

4A 4A for a reason, for a reason,
none at all.

DEATHDOUBLEDACTYL

Cheerier, merrier,
Death came today to claim
My pit bull terrier—
She had been lame.
We cannot bury her
Under the window frame—
Necrobacteria,
It is to blame.

Parasitic Twin

There is a cold spot in my head.
Like a drop of mercury it rolls downward
Through cracks in my brain, settles in its caverns,
And coats their walls like ice on the back of an athlete.

Nodding, I experience the following:
My shoulder is tapped.
I turn. Nothing.
The shoulder gets tapped again. Quickly
I glance back—a black figure furtively escapes behind a green curtain
Behind which it whistles and trembles
I pull it back.
                    A new image. Twisted, scary.

I awaken
Drained, my heart slowing to normal
                                        and slower.

Am I okay?
Is it futile (for far-flung desire to transfix me in waking hours
Or to shatter the windows to pleasure and grab it boldly)?

You say you're not sure.
It *is* rude and probably illegal
And anyway it's crazy.

THE GLOVE

He circles the parcel he's laid out in the foyer.
        She walks to the mailbox.
He looks at the postmark.
        She finds a small envelope.
He knows that she sent it.
        It is from him she thinks, biting her lip.
        The lip blanches. The envelope is
        Manila and tiny like the one a teacher
        Once sent her home with her tooth in.
He eyes the package suspiciously — it is several
Meters long but only as thick as a woman's arm and
Wrapped in butcher block paper.
        She takes it inside. The baby is crying.
He touches his belt instinctively and
Walks around the package. He touches it with his toe.
        She sits down. She crosses her legs,
        She uncrosses them and stands up and then
        Sits back down again and removes the white cotton
        Glove she wears when her eczema is acting up and
        Places it next to her, there on the couch.
He stoops and hoists the cylindrical package to his lap.
He remembers a promise he once broke. He tears at the paper
        She sneezes.
        When two people love each other,
        And one of them betrays the other,
        The mind of the betrayed trembles
        On its coatrack, and the betrayer's
        Heart tries to exit its cupboard, and
        The betrayer's hand reaches for the
        Betrayer's eyes but the betrayer
        Stops short of gouging them out.
He cuts through some tape. His heart pounds
As if it wants some door to open. He pulls
Back the wrapping. A white pole is exposed.

She opens the envelope, applies pressure
To its sides, and dumps into her hand
First an eyelash and then a small white
Piece of paper with symbols on it.
The pole is long and delicate, too delicate
To support a birdhouse or to hang coats on.
On the piece of paper, a blue-inked arrow
Meets a barrier. Centimeters away is its
Mirror image: a barrier meets a tiny arrow.
The pole is too long to be a cane, too brittle
To vault from. He stares at it and puts it under
His nose. Should he break it? Should he thank
Her? He does not know. He will never guess
It is the ten foot pole with which she would
Never touch him.
She examines the piece of paper seated
In her cracked palm. She cannot bathe
The baby today. She is not many green
Stamps from a Seal-a-Meal. This
Small piece of paper she holds
Represents the inch of her life
Within which he will beat her
If she ever tells her mother (his wife.)

The Trial

People have got things backwards, willfully:
The soldier in the paper is not a hero
"The men and women blah blah blah" are not brave—
To kill in war takes no courage, only servility.
Courage can be found instead in an adjacent news item
About the "monster and a coward" who slew his wife and children.
Against the laws of conscience, church, and state he acted
Dismissing civility, sanity—"something snapped"—What courage!
To face hatred and hell, to reject everything at all, to give his life,
His children, his wife, to be so ridiculously corrupt to be marked,
Disdained by even God, to make one's own war: oneself v. that which isn't.

In "legitimate" war there are no such stakes—one has everything to gain
And, what's more, no choice about it anyway.

                              The brave man is the one who
Slew half a dozen girl scouts (one particularly pretty with important parents
Photographed with a pet on the penultimate day of her life is burned into my
Memory via television). He isn't the one who, with aplomb, dropped
Some artillery mistakenly on some bomb shelter, killing civilians—
(Brown, foreign girl scouts no doubt among them.)

                              He is that one
Who set fire to his son ("to shut his wife's big mouth"—yes, go figure),
Not the one who killed men with whom he'd never argued because ordered
Only to be rewarded with a little
                    Friendly
                       Fire.

By now we've learned that courage is an amoral quality;
Lesson 2 is about compassion. Say you're on the jury
Of the Girl Scout Gouger and sick with fury—
You've seen the famous photo of the cute, rich one and her rabbit, Murray.
And you've seen the after photo, the gore, the horror!

"The poor dear, oh! and her parents! He shall hang, I assure!"
That is what compassion isn't if compassion is to be something special.
To gaze upon the defendant, his head in his hands—he's chuckling—
And feel a tidal wave of love for him is far more rare;
As the verdict is handed down and a hush goes through the poisoned air.

The Ravens

on the patio outside my hotel room in Cancun
dither around a plastic container of roast piglet
from the Commercial Mexicana
left out for the cat.
One raven strips a strip of meat free
Another snatches it from the first's beak
A third swoops down. A fourth and a fifth
fight over a morsel. Two ravens
tumble away from the center and fight
forgetting the piglet. Each is loud.
They circle. They peck.
There is far more hunger than there is piglet.
The sun shines on a fracas of oily
black plumes.

      By now
the sharp undergraduate should recognize
I am writing about something other than ravens.
Do they represent death?
Nevermore.
Do they represent women?
                  Well, women *are* like ravens—
their competitiveness,
their attraction to shiny objects—
going berserk over gewgaws and gems—
I've never understood this about women;
jewelry does not make them more beautiful—
(I've always been most impressed
by She of the Unadorned Neck.)
Not that I'm out of touch with my feminine side.
I know what it's like to be a woman—
I've been raped in prison—my teeth knocked out,
my anus gushing blood.
I have also noticed, as doubtless countless women have,

how a man on the beach can look promising from the back—
muscular, broad shoulders, nicely-shaped can—
but can be positively revolting seen from the front—
ugly face, old, too hairy, fat stomach.
But no, the ravens clawing one another are not women.
They are poets
scrambling stupidly
over a tiny pie.
They gossip, they grab, they grant-apply, they go
to the University of Iowa. Each is loud
their shiny eyes full of black ideas.
This is why I am calling for the slaughter of poets.
We must assassinate them at readings,
hunt them down in coffeehouses,
spray them with bullets as they leave their apartments,
defenestrate them from their offices and classrooms.
We must stuff their books down their throats.
"We have no mercy here!"
We must reopen Auschwitz.

Except, the birds weren't really ravens.
They were black but much smaller.
And I've increased their numbers
and their wickedness
for effect. And I lied:
There was plenty of piglet for everyone.

Poets are no different from anybody else.
We are like bulls in a ring, confused and dying
to ridiculous music.
We are like Frankenstein's monster wandering Antarctica
wondering why, *why*? Our Creator has turned on us.
In any case, we are all of us sinners.

But here is something that really happened:
Yesterday an aviary collapsed in the Bronx
releasing 33 exotic birds—
whose names I do not know—
into the frigid air.
Last night I dreamed of dying, until
I awoke to find a strange woman standing in my room.
She wandered out the door and onto the roof
when I picked up the phone.

This morning I looked among the pigeons
for a bird that didn't fit in.
What if poetry doesn't matter?
What if they all freeze or get killed by meaner birds?
What if I called the police on an angel?
As they say in the song, "I'm a no-good coward..."
And this is my swan song. I will never write poetry again.